FUTURISTIC
LEADERSHIP

A→Z

Daily Desktop Reference
for 21st Century
Executives & Entrepreneurs

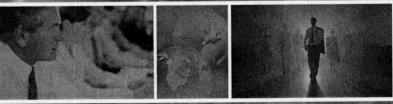

FRANK FEATHER

FUTURISTIC LEADERSHIP A→Z

**Daily Desktop Reference
for 21st Century
Executives & Entrepreneurs**

© 2004, Frank Feather
www.future-trends.com

Distributed by:  Inspire Media
MOTIVATION FOR EVERYONE

Published by: *Motivated Publishing Ventures*

ISBN: 0-9736187-2-8
1st Printing, September 2004

For Sarah

Best wishes!

I have no fear of the future.
Let us go forward into its mysteries,
let us tear aside the veils which hide it
from our eyes, and let us move onwards
with confidence and courage
—Winston S. Churchill

TABLE OF CONTENTS

Personal Message from Frank Feather

About this Book...
and How to Use It

THIS A-Z DAILY DESKTOP REFERENCE has **a common thread**. The focus is not routine leadership but futuristic leadership. And there's a big difference between them.

Leadership is not a job title. Leaders routinely hold executive positions, but routine leaders rarely renew organizations to attain fresh success in an ever-changing world. Routine leaders tend to manage the status quo and thus fall behind what the ever-changing operating environment demands.

By contrast, futuristic leaders stay well ahead of the trends and simply make the future happen. And how they accomplish that is summed up in the A-Z contents of this book.

Standard A-Z Content Structure

Futuristic leadership is explored in 26 keyword sections. Each word is presented in 4 pages of succinct text, organized in a standard format for all 26 words, as follows:

1. **Futuristic Meaning**: The word is defined both in futuristic terms and as a verb, an action word. Futuristic leaders are verbs - they do things.

2. **Inspirational Quotations to Inspire You**: A page full of inspirational quotes by famous leaders or authorities about the chosen verb.

3. **Futuristic Leadership Principle**: The word's futuristic leadership principle is pointedly stated and very briefly explained.

4. **Example and Application**: A real-world example of the leadership verb is given, and its application is elaborated upon for tomorrow's business world.

5. **Questions to Ask**: The section on each word concludes by prompting some ideas for you to brainstorm, with space to add more of your own pertinent questions.

About the Exemplars

As listed in the Table of Contents next to each word, the exemplar for each verb usually is a recognized leader (individual or organization) that best exemplifies that verb; that is, the characteristic for which that person or organization is most generally recognized.

However, in reading each example, you will find that most (if not all) of them exhibit most (if not all) of the characteristics of the 26 A-Z verbs. They are complete, holistic leaders: some were the futuristic leaders of their time; others are the futuristic leaders of today and tomorrow.

Use this Book Daily

Thanks to the book's A-Z structure, you can dip in and out of the easy-to-read short chapters whenever they appeal to you or as your leadership needs arise.

I strongly suggest you keep a copy handy, out on your desk, and refer to it daily. Take a few minutes at the start of each day to read and think about one verb and refresh your own futuristic leadership ability. Each time you do so, I know you'll see things differently. It also will remind you to wear your "futuristic leadership" hat - always.

Keeping this book on your desk, where your colleagues will see it, also will make a strong statement about you, your futuristic leadership approach, and the organization you lead - and about what is expected of them also.

In fact, I suggest you expose your people to this book's content. A key responsibility of futuristic leaders is to duplicate themselves and groom the next generation of futuristic leaders. Indeed, that's the only way you will leave a complete and lasting legacy.

Every best wish for your
futuristic leadership success!

FRANK FEATHER

June 2004

Preface

"SEE" THE FUTURE...
THE A-Z OF IT

FUTURISTIC LEADERS literally "see" the **future and make it happen.** They enable others to see it, motivate them to venture there, lead them there, reward them when they get there, and celebrate their collective success. They are true leaders who understand the A-Z of winning the future.

Futuristic leaders **A**CHIEVE results because they truly **B**ELIEVE a different future is possible. They **C**HANGE their own and their organization's behavior, habits, and culture, in order to obtain their collective **D**REAM.

Futuristic leaders fully **E**XPECT to reach their goal - and also fully "expect the unexpected" along the way - because they unswervingly **F**OCUS on that goal.

Aware that reaching the future requires that they and their organizations **G**ROW - both mentally and

5

spiritually - futuristic leaders **H**EAR things: they listen intently for clues and pieces of vital information that will guide them in that growth.

Futuristic leaders vividly **I**MAGINE what the future will be like, what needs to change to get there, and how the charted course might need to vary along the route.

They **J**USTIFY their mission, not only based on profitable returns, but in the proper ethics and values that will bring it to fruition.

Futuristic leaders **K**NOW both what they know and what they don't know, and what more they and their teams will still need to know in the future. They constantly **L**EARN, day by day, decision by decision, as they move forward.

Futuristic leaders **M**OTIVATE themselves, and inspire those around them to do the same, to adventurously **N**AVIGATE previously uncharted territory. They **O**RGANIZE and optimize every available capacity and resource to help them **P**ERSEVERE until every part of the mission is accomplished.

Futuristic leaders always **Q**UESTION their advisors, their information, and themselves. Then they can best **R**ESPOND to challenges and opportunities in ways that **S**TRATEGIZE the most responsible and best possible future outcomes.

Futuristic leaders **T**EACH everything they know to the highest-qualified teams of individuals. They **U**PLIFT them to **V**ISUALIZE and drive towards their collective future.

As well, in today's "webolutionary" Internet Age, futuristic leaders encourage their teams to literally **W**EBIFY their organizations into value-creating networks, or "biznets."

Futuristic leaders also **X**EROGRAPH themselves: they "clone" or duplicate their own abilities and processes in others, to ensure ongoing growth and continuity through yet another generation of futuristic leaders.

Finally, futuristic leaders repeatedly **Y**IELD consistent and spectacular results, and **Z**OOM their organizations speedily to ever-succeeding peaks of success.

As already noted in my opening "Personal Message," there are obvious interconnections between these 26 verbs. Futuristic leadership is a dynamic A-Z synergy of seeing the whole future - and then making it happen in the most expeditious and responsible way.

FUTURISTIC
LEADERSHIP A→Z

WHAT IS
FUTURISTIC LEADERSHIP?

**There are three kinds of people:
those who make things happen,
those who watch things happen, and
those who wonder what happened.**
— *James Lovell (NASA astronaut)*

**You can't manage change.
You can only be ahead of it.**
— *Peter Drucker (management guru)*

ONLY THE FUTURE IS MANAGEABLE, due
to three inescapable reasons. First, you
can't manage the past: it's over and done
with. You can only change a prior decision by
making a new decision sometime from now.

No, you can't manage the present either. The present is a mere nanosecond of time as we constantly
move from the past to the future.

You can only manage "what hasn't happened yet" -

the future. Leadership is about steering your organization into that ever-new future.

Of course, otherwise-logical people protest that you logically can't predict the future. They say the future can't be known. That's because the future defies purely logical thinking. Instead, it comes logically to the intuitive rather than the linear mind. You can "see" the future.

How Can You "See" the Future?

The "unknown" future can become "known" quite clearly by whole-brained futuristic leaders. They see its wholeness - the big picture - and how it fits together and how trends interact.

Futuristic leaders literally "see" the future and then "map" how to get there. They have a clear idea of what the future will be like.

It's not magic or crystal-ball gazing; they have a genuine feel for relevant trends and their outcome. True leaders are futurists.

Jigsaw Puzzle of the Future

Futurists constantly try to assemble a jigsaw puzzle of the future. You never have all the pieces, so the picture is never complete. In fact, each morning you'll find some pieces (that you put in the jigsaw as recently as last night) are in the wrong place and you need to re-think things.

Futuristic leaders take minute-to-minute decisions based on that iterative jigsaw puzzle, which they keep at the forefront of their minds. Their never-completed jigsaw puzzle is a constantly changing focus board. No, that is not a contradiction. Christopher Columbus found the New World by using a very speculative map.

Their evolving jigsaw puzzle helps futuristic leaders navigate the uncharted territory of their organization's future. Their jigsaw puzzle is their "map" to their "new world" - a future which they see most vividly, and which they set out to reach as expeditiously as possible.

Futuristic Leaders Stand in the Future

In the end, it's not so much what will happen but what you do about it. As noted earlier, futuristic leaders are doers; they achieve things. They are verbs.

Futuristic leaders don't tip-toe into the future; they stride boldly forward, guided by trends. In fact, they always plant one foot in the future. They regularly stand in the future, take a good look around, scout the best options, and feel comfortable there. They virtually live there.

Futuristic Leaders Are Time Travelers

Futuristic leaders traverse a past-present-future time continuum, constantly shifting perspective along that continuum. They surf across the sweep of time, creating change and making strategic decisions about how best to navigate their organization's optimal future.

So what's going on in your organization's future?

- Based on where you are now, what does your future look like?
- What are you doing about it?
- What will your organization do about it?
- How would you like things to be different?
- How can you make things different?
- What is your "map" to your new world?

This book will prompt many such questions.

Use this book to take a realistic look at the various leadership options for your organization. Make the best one happen, and I guarantee you'll leave a true legacy of futuristic leadership.

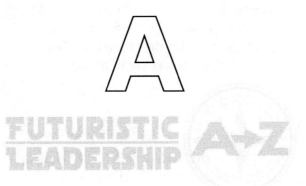

ACHIEVE

FUTURISTIC MEANING

To bring to a perfected future state. To carry to a final close. To accomplish or perform a feat, exploit, or enterprise. To obtain or gain, as the result of exertion. To finish. To win.

Similar to: Accomplish, fulfill, complete, execute, perform, realize, obtain.

Opposites: Blow it, choke, fail, fall short, lose, miss, quit.

QUOTATIONS to INSPIRE YOU
to
ACHIEVE

**Destiny is not a matter of chance;
it is a matter of choice.
It is not to be waited for;
it is to be achieved.**
— *William Jennings Bryan (politician)*

**There is nothing that cannot be
achieved by firm imagination.**
— *Japanese Proverb*

I want to put a ding in the universe.
— *Steve Jobs (Apple Computer)*

**Those who dare to fail miserably,
can achieve greatly.**
— *John F. Kennedy (35th US President)*

**When one door closes another opens;
but we often look so long and so
regretfully upon the closed door,
that we do not see the ones
which open for us.**
— *Alexander Graham Bell (inventor)*

FUTURISTIC LEADERSHIP PRINCIPLE

The future belongs to those who get there first - to those who achieve.

The word "achieve" comes from the French "achever" (to finish) and "chef" (chief). In short, chiefs finish things. Each of us has an innate need to achieve, but true leaders achieve their goals before others - and finish what they start.

EXAMPLE & APPLICATION

We don't know what we're capable of until we envision ourselves out of our existing situation.

Raised on a poor farm by her grandmother, who taught her to read at age 3, Oprah Winfrey is the first African-American woman billionaire.

The ability to read launched her career: she began reciting readings at church, and her books revealed new life options. Watching her grandmother boiling clothes one day (they had no washing machine) she had a vision of the need to change her life.

Challenged by her father to be an "A" student, she became an honors grad. She also became a radio announcer while still in high school and a TV anchor while still attending university.

By 1985, at age 31, she had the Oprah Show with a 20+ million world audience, her own production company Harpo, an Oscar nomination in movies, and was planning her book club and magazine.

Oprah changed her life and, in turn, views her calling as helping other people change their lives. She says that only by accepting your life can you change it, and that success

15

is about reaching the point where you are comfortable with yourself and your role in life.

In 1998, Time magazine named her one of the most influential people of the century. In 2001, she was chosen to co-host the memorial service at Yankee Stadium for the 9/11 victims. In 2004, Wharton business school named her one of the most influential business people of the last 25 years. Her production company generates $314 million in annual revenues.

These and many other achievements are a story of steely determination to change her lot in life, an unswerving focus, and a selfless approach to helping others to do likewise.

To achieve your goals, force yourself out of your comfort zone, realistically access your present situation and future possibilities, and you will achieve them. Set your priority and go for it.

QUESTIONS to ASK

- How achievement-oriented am I?
- How about our organization?
- What do we feel most passionate about?
- What's the #1 priority for us to achieve?
- What will we look like when it's done?

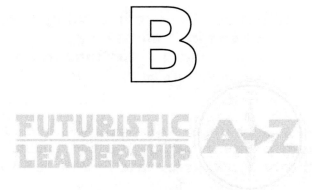

BELIEVE

FUTURISTIC MEANING

To be convinced, approaching certainty - upon evidence of reasons, arguments, and deductions - that a true state of affairs exists or will occur in the future, and will prove beneficial.

Similar to: Convinced, certain, sure.

Opposites: Doubt, distrust, suspect.

QUOTATIONS to INSPIRE YOU
to
BELIEVE

When you believe in a thing,
believe in it all the way,
implicitly and unquestionably.
— *Walt Disney (Disney Company)*

It is not so much what you believe in,
as the way in which you believe it,
and proceed to translate it into action.
— *Lin Yutang (philosopher)*

If you believe you can,
or if you believe you can't,
you are probably right.
— *Henry Ford (Ford Motor Co)*

"One can't believe impossible things,"
said Alice.
"I daresay you haven't had much practice,"
said the Queen.
"When I was your age,
I always did it for half-an-hour a day.
Why, sometimes I've believed
as many as six impossible things
before breakfast."
— *Lewis Carroll (author)*

FUTURISTIC LEADERSHIP PRINCIPLE

Believe deep down, and it will come true.

People who hold strong beliefs are more likely to act on them and to make them happen. When you believe you can do it, your creative mind will show you how.

EXAMPLE and APPLICATION

None of us know what we're truly capable of, especially when others don't believe something is possible.

> **Roger Bannister believed he could run a mile in less than four minutes. While conventional wisdom said it couldn't be done, as a university athlete and medical doctor, he believed it could.**
>
> He practiced repeatedly with pace-making teammates - timed lap after timed lap, trial race after trial race - and then broke the 4-minute barrier.
>
> Within a few months, several other athletes also achieved what Bannister first proved possible.

Belief acts like a built-in thermostat on today's action, regulating what you achieve tomorrow:

— If you believe the challenge is scary, tough and likely impossible, then it will be.

— If you believe the challenge is exciting, easy, and highly possible, then it will be.

To do the impossible, believe that you can. Say to yourself, "I'm positive I can," and you will then see how to do it. Repeat your belief over and over until it becomes embedded and alters how you think and behave.

Then rehearse how you will bring it to fruition. Practice it and pace yourself for the final attempt. Each attempt will reinforce your belief.

Do some experimenting. Undertake pilot projects until you work all the "bugs" out and get the process running smoothly. Keep doing that until you get it right.

Prove the skeptics wrong. Then roll the changes out, organization wide. Just go out and create a big break-through success.

QUESTIONS to ASK

- How clear am I about what I believe?
- How firmly do I believe?
- How well does our organization believe?
- What will it be like when we do believe it?
- What will convince us? (Write it down and marshal the evidence for it.)

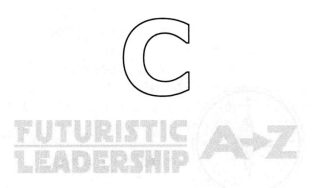

CHANGE

FUTURISTIC MEANING

To alter, become different in essence. To lose one's original nature; to transform. To abandon old ways for more-favorable methods. To change the pace and direction of activity.

Similar to: Alter, vary, deviate, substitute, innovate, diversify, shift, veer, turn, reverse, mutate, transition, revolt.

Opposites: Continue, hold, remain, stay, fossilize, freeze up.

QUOTATIONS to INSPIRE YOU
to
CHANGE

**Change is the law of life,
and those who look only
to the past or present
are certain to miss the future.**
— *John F. Kennedy (35th US President)*

**Be the change you want
to see in the world.**
— *Mahatma Gandhi (pacifist)*

**The human mind,
once stretched by a new idea,
never regains its original dimensions.**
— *Oliver Wendell Holmes (jurist)*

**If you've always done it that way,
it's probably wrong.**
— *Charles Kettering (inventor)*

**I want a lot of men
who have an infinite capacity
to not know what can't be done.**
— *Henry Ford (Ford Motor Co)*

FUTURISTIC LEADERSHIP PRINCIPLE

If you do what you've always done, you'll get what you've always got.

To change means to make something different and preferable from what exists. To change, you must break out of today's mythically-limiting and intractable options.

EXAMPLE and APPLICATION

Futuristic leaders are the first to initiate change, the first to make a move, to test a new idea.

In the face of much derision, Arthur C. Clarke, the space futurist, created the idea of geo-stationary orbit communication satellites.

As a result of that and other experiences, he often pointed out that new ideas pass through three stages:

1. It can't be done;
2. It probably can be done, but it's not worth doing; and
3. I knew it was a good idea all along!

Other than our planet and its natural resources, everything in this world stems from a creative idea that was then acted upon. Creativity is all about novel options, about thinking afresh, and then turning the idea into reality.

Futuristic leaders let go of outmoded certainties. They shake their kaleidoscopes and re-vision what's possible. They take things apart and re-assemble them in a future-relevant way.

To change, then, you don't re-invent the wheel, but you may well have to re-invent the vehicle. And never fear to rock the boat. Change doesn't happen until after the boat rocks. Rock it!

To change the boat's direction, everybody must row in unison towards the future. If not, replace personnel and managers with those who don't obstruct but who will initiate futuristic change.

Then give them a humungous challenge that blows their minds and turns on their creative afterburners.

QUESTIONS to ASK

- How change-oriented am I?
- Which personal habit can I change today?
- How change-oriented is our organization?
- What will happen if things don't change?
- What humungous change can we make this year?
- What will happen once that happens?

DREAM

FUTURISTIC MEANING

To anticipate a cherished desire.
To let the mind run; to imagine and envision a wonderful objective. To develop a visionary scheme that is not merely a dream, but a very realistic aim.

Similar to: Aspire, fantasize, revel, delight, ambition, desire.

Opposites: Nightmare, spook, dash.

QUOTATIONS to INSPIRE YOU
to
DREAM

We grow by dreams.
All big men are dreamers.
— *Woodrow T. Wilson (28th US President)*

If you advance confidently in the
direction of your dreams, and endeavor
to live the life you have imagined,
you will meet with unexpected success.
— *Henry David Thoreau (author)*

A goal is a dream with a deadline.
Cherish your visions and your dreams,
as they are the children of your soul, the
blueprints of your ultimate achievement.
— *Napoleon Hill (motivational author)*

If you can dream it, you can do it.
— *Walt Disney (Disney Company)*

You see things and you say "Why?"
But I dream things that never were;
and I say "Why not?"
— *George Bernard Shaw (playwright)*

FUTURISTIC LEADERSHIP PRINCIPLE

Nothing is as durable as a realistic dream with a reasonable deadline.

The world may change as you pursue your dream, but a realistic dream will not. Changing conditions and responsibilities will not erase it. And the gloomiest naysayer will never dissuade you from pursuing it.

EXAMPLE and APPLICATION

Futuristic leaders dare to dream. And they dream big - very big. They are headstrong in purpose and the pursuit of their goals.

World War II fighter pilot Douglas Bader never abandoned his dream of being a flying ace.

Bader lost both legs in an aerobatic stunt which went badly wrong. Told he wouldn't walk again, never mind fly, he mastered artificial limbs, trained to fly again, re-applied to the RAF, was accepted, and entered the war as a Squadron Leader.

Later shot down over Germany, he was able to bail out of his crashing plane only by removing one of his artificial legs, which was trapped.

He escaped his captors, returned to England a war hero, trained many more pilots, and finally retired as a much-decorated Group Captain.

Don't let the dream stealers cut you off at the knees and take away your dream. They always reject any possibility of things being different or better. Kick any dream stealers off your team. They are a night-mare to have around.

Replace dream stealers with a team of dream weavers and dream catchers. Encourage them to dream about an ambitious future for your organization to achieve. Then equip them with the tools and training to make it happen.

Don't let temporary setbacks and necessary course-corrections derail you. Never lose sight of your dream. Remain steadfast and unshaken and pursue it constantly.

QUESTIONS to ASK

- How clear and ambitious is my dream?
- What is my fondest business ambition?
- How dream-oriented is our team?
- What stirs our hearts and emotions?
- We need an organization which … … …
- What specific steps can we take today, this week, that will move us closer to our dream?
- What will happen, once that happens?

EXPECT

FUTURISTIC MEANING

To regard as almost certain to happen.
To fully expect something to occur. Also to consider a future event or outcome as obligatory. Can also mean to expect the unexpected.

Similar to: Anticipate, look for, await.

Opposites: Doubt, disbelieve.

QUOTATIONS to INSPIRE YOU
to
EXPECT

**High expectations
are the key to everything.**
— *Sam Walton (Wal-Mart)*

**The little that is completed,
vanishes from the sight
of one who looks forward
to what is still to do.**
— *Johann Wolfgang von Goethe (playwright)*

**Whatever we expect with confidence
becomes our own self-fulfilling prophecy.**
— *Brian Tracy (motivational author)*

**I can't imagine going on
when there are no more expectations.**
— *Dame Edith Evans (actress)*

**If you accept the expectations of others,
especially negative ones,
then you never will change the outcome.**
— *Michael Jordon (NBA Superstar)*

FUTURISTIC LEADERSHIP PRINCIPLE

To achieve the future, expect it.

Expectations come from a mental act or thought process that always refers to the future, to some coming event that you consider is almost certain to occur - just like death and taxes.

EXAMPLE and APPLICATION

Futuristic leaders expect things to turn out well, and have confidence in their ability to make it so. They operate "as if" it had already happened.

Dag Hammarskjöld, the second UN Secretary-General, believed and expected that the UN had a limitless capacity to wage peace, provided it was properly led.

Always setting high expectations, he won the 1961 Nobel Peace Prize posthumously, having died that year in a plane crash, leading yet another UN peace mission, this time in war-ravaged Congo.

He positioned the UN as the world peacekeeper at the height of the Cold War. Using what he called "intense diplomacy for unconventional and novel experiments," he was the architect of basic rules and principles of global diplomacy which led him to negotiate many unexpected peace treaties.

Futuristic leaders tend to achieve more than what they realistically expect. Don't fool yourself with false hopes or over-expectations. But positive expectations will reflect back on you and let you achieve miracles.

Always expect excellence and push your team toward it. Intensely believe and expect the best outcome. Expect obstacles and opportunities, but fully expect to meet and overcome them as they arise. Rehearse their occurrence and "reverse analyze" what to do beforehand.

Always try to exceed people's expectations. To learn what they expect, simply ask them. The better you clarify everybody's expectations - internal and external to your organization - the better are the chances of overall success.

Also expect resistance. The best ideas generate most resistance because they entail disruption. People don't like their routine upset. They don't like surprises. So anticipate the change: what will differ, what might go wrong, how people will benefit, and what they might have to give up.

Then discuss and rehearse it with them so they will become part of the change and will embrace it because they see, and buy into, its benefits.

QUESTIONS to ASK

- How expectant am I?
- How expectant is our organization?
- What outcome do we want and expect?
- What do our customers expect?
- How do we satisfy those expectations?

FOCUS

FUTURISTIC MEANING

To concentrate and sustain - with maximum clarity and distinction - attention, energy, and emphasis, on a central future objective.
To bring ideas and emotions into sharp focus, and converge or concentrate them on a central point. To focalize.

Similar to: Clarify, center, rivet.

Opposites: Blur, dilute, distract.

QUOTATIONS to INSPIRE YOU
to
FOCUS

**Concentrate all your thoughts.
The sun's rays do not burn
until brought to a focus.**
— *Alexander Graham Bell (inventor)*

**Chase two rabbits and you catch neither.
To achieve much, do one thing at a time.**
— *Chinese Proverb*

**The secret of effectiveness is concentration.
Effective executives do first things first
and they do one thing at a time.**
— *Peter F. Drucker (management guru)*

**I never hit a shot, not even in practice,
without having a very sharp, in-focus
picture of it in my head.**
— *Jack Nicklaus (master golfer)*

**With practice and focus,
you can extend yourself far more
than you ever believed possible.**
— *Edmund Hillary (mountaineer)*

FUTURISTIC LEADERSHIP PRINCIPLE

Pursue the future with laser-like focus. Allow no distractions.

Constantly focus on the primary aim, and you will attain unprecedented goals. When goal-oriented people adopt a leader's inspiring goal - all aiming in the same direction and making course corrections to maintain progress - they make stunning achievements.

EXAMPLE and APPLICATION

Focused leaders look for what needs doing and will have an impact on the world.

NASA's complex, decade-long Apollo mission had a simple 7-word focus:

"Perform a manned lunar landing and return."

When JFK set the goal to put a man on the moon and bring him back safely within a decade, the project's very size and complexity made all other previous human pioneering endeavors pale, and everyday projects seem easy.

Going to the moon was the ultimate undertaking. Apollo took billions of dollars, millions of hours of time, and the skills of thousands of people.

But that team kept its 7-word focus until Armstrong stepped on the moon and later returned safely to Earth.

Future-focused leaders and teams intuitively know why and how they do what they do. It is second nature to them. They know what needs to be done and concentrate on its outcome.

Interestingly, the word focus comes from the Latin *foci*, meaning "hearth" or "fireplace."

Focused people feel at home with big challenges, they catch the spark, get fired up - but not mesmerized - by the opportunity they see dancing in those flames, and never ever take their eye off the over-riding goal.

No matter how long it takes, they concentrate and never get distracted. People who can't focus are easily drawn into diversions. They waste time, energy and resources on stuff that has nothing to do with the over-arching goal. Fuzzy about the future, their enthusiasm soon wanes.

Future-focused people beat them every time.

QUESTIONS to ASK

- How well focused am I?
- How well focused is our organization?
- What will matter most in a decade?
- What is our moon?
- How do we get there, and by when?

GROW

FUTURISTIC MEANING

To spring up and flourish. To become larger, greater, or bigger. To expand or gain. To increase in size by natural process. To cause to grow or develop, and to reach maturity.

Similar to: Raise, cultivate, extend, flower, blossom, re-seed.

Opposites: Decline, diminish, shrink, shrivel, recede, die.

QUOTATIONS to INSPIRE YOU
to
GROW

Do it. Try it. Fix it. Grow it.
— *Sam Walton (Wal-Mart)*

**Unless you try to do something
beyond what you have mastered,
you will never grow.**
— *C. R. Lawton*

**Enough shovels of earth
- a mountain.
Enough pails of water
- a river.**
— *Chinese Proverb*

**No man ever steps in
the same river twice,
for it's not the same river
and he's not the same man.**
— *Heraclitus (philosopher)*

Grow or die. Eat or get eaten.
— *Anonymous*

FUTURISTIC LEADERSHIP PRINCIPLE

Record growth needs "growth" leadership.

Think like an oak, not an acorn. Growth leaders seek to do things better and are never afraid to experiment. Always thinking about how to grow faster, they set audacious, humungous goals.

EXAMPLE and APPLICATION

Growth leaders spot where trends are going in their industry, even in mature markets, and head there before competitors wake up.

Wal-Mart has sustained the most dramatic rate of growth in world business history. This is thanks to its founder's growth mindset - a mindset that built a leadership legacy which outlives him.

Sam Walton, student council president and state champion quarterback, was a leader driven to grow to succeed. He started out as a JC Penney sales clerk and learned everything he could about retail.

He quit that in 1945 to open Walton's, a small shop, and did $72,000 in sales that year. Always pushing growth - "test, promote, change" - Walton grew sales 29% a year until 1962, when he opened a brand new self-service store - the first Wal-Mart.

In 1977, with 38 stores, he set a $1 billion sales goal. In 1990, at $40 billion in sales, he aimed to triple that to $125 billion by 2000 - a goal reached two years early, but which he didn't live to see.

Under its new "growth leader" David Glass, Wal-Mart now does $1 billion in sales a day! While its competitors struggle, Wal-Mart is #1 and still grows rapidly. If Wal-Mart maintains its meteoric growth rate, sales will top $1 trillion by 2010 - the first trillion dollar company - and it will employ 5 million people worldwide.

Wal-Mart became #1 by driving costs out of its industry. That cut profit margins, so Walton grew sales at a relentless pace, opening ever more stores and installing computer systems to keep track of everything.

You will achieve humungous goals when enlightened "growth leadership" shows the way.

QUESTIONS to ASK

- How can I raise my "growth" quotient?
- How do we develop a growth culture?
- What growth rate will outpace others?
- What humungous goal can we set?
  Is it audacious enough?

HEAR

FUTURISTIC MEANING

To truly listen and pay attention to trends. To keep your ear to the ground. To get to know, become aware of. To examine or hear evidence. To give audience to. To heed. To acknowledge.

Similar to: Listen, get wind of, pick up on, find out, take in, to "get it."

Opposites: Ignore, misunderstand, misread, don't "get it."

QUOTATIONS to INSPIRE YOU
to
HEAR

**We really listen to our users.
Some of the best ideas at eBay
come from our community.**
— *Meg Whitman (eBay)*

**No one ever listened
themselves out of a job.**
— *Calvin Coolidge (13th US President)*

**Lay thine ear close to the ground and
... hear the tread of travelers.**
— *William Shakespeare (playwright)*

**Listen long enough
and the person will
generally come up
with a solution.**
— *Mary Kay Ash (Mary Kay)*

**Hear one side and
you will be in the dark.
Hear both and all will be clear.**
— *Lord Chesterfield (UK politician)*

FUTURISTIC LEADERSHIP PRINCIPLE

Keep your ear to the ground to hear the future approach, and then lead toward it.

Also hear what customers say they want. Don't tell them what they need, ask them. And help them figure out what they will need tomorrow.

EXAMPLE and APPLICATION

Billions of dollars in business opportunities are lost each year for lack of careful listening.

> **Global internet trading phenomenon eBay really listens to and hears its community of users.**
>
> CEO Meg Whitman says many of eBay's best ideas come from users, with whom it communicates frequently to learn what they want.
>
> Examples are the feedback profile on merchants, the Personal Shopper concept, the eBay Life Newsletter, and the ability to separate transaction-related feedback from non-transaction feedback.
>
> Whitman says users think of things that eBay should do, far better and faster than the company, because they are "living it" on a day-to-day basis.

Futuristic leaders constantly seek feedback from associates and clients. Really listen to what they need. If you don't hear them, you die.

You have 2 eyes, 2 ears, 1 mouth. Use them in that ratio. Listen up! Listen up, you hear?!

Leading minds listen and hear; small minds monop-
olize talking and hear nothing. You may hear it, but
are you listening? You may listen, but are you hearing? Hearing means being attentive to what's truly
being said.

Withhold judgment on what you hear until you hear
it all and confirm what was really said. Listen to
ideas as if you are later to present them in detail to
another group. Summarize what you heard, plus
what they didn't say. Ask them to confirm that you
heard correctly.

Don't filter what you don't want to hear. Often,
throwaway remarks reveal the best clues. So listen
to many voices, including your own inner voice. And
step outside yourself. Be the fly on the wall. Put
yourself in other people's shoes and imagine what
they are thinking.

The more people feel you hear them, the more they
too will evolve as leaders who hear. Listen for words
like "I believe" and "I recommend." Always ask
people what they recommend. If they never recommend anything, fire them.

QUESTIONS to ASK

- How well do I listen? Do I truly hear?
- How well does our organization hear?
- What new feedback tools do we need?

IMAGINE

FUTURISTIC MEANING

To contrive, devise, or design a future.
To form a mental image or conception of something not present, or that does not yet exist. To conceive of, or envisage. To form a notion in the mind. To compass; to purpose. To have insight about.

Similar to: Suppose, reckon, guess, intuit.

Opposites: Draw a mental blank.

QUOTATIONS to INSPIRE YOU
to
IMAGINE

**The stronger your imagination,
the more variegated your universe.**
— *Winston S. Churchill (UK Prime Minister)*

**The world belongs to those who
cross many bridges in their imagination
before others see even a single bridge.**
— *Chinese Proverb*

**Perceptions are important,
but they make a poor
substitute for insight.**
— *Phil Knight (Nike)*

**Microsoft is a company
that manages imagination.**
— *Bill Gates (Microsoft)*

**Disneyland will never be completed.
It will continue to grow as long as there
is imagination left in the world.**
— *Walt Disney (Disney Company)*

FUTURISTIC LEADERSHIP PRINCIPLE

If you can imagine it, then it is possible.

Futuristic leaders stretch minds to imagine previously unimaginable projects for their organizations. They "imagineer" the future.

EXAMPLE and APPLICATION

"Imagineering" is a term coined by Walt Disney to combine imagination with engineering.

Disney literally conjures up the future of family fun and has an uncanny ability to tap into our deepest desires.

In 1952, Walt Disney asked a few of his best animators to develop an idea for a new kind of amusement park, Disneyland. The group came to be known as the Imagineering unit.

Imagineering is Disney's master planning, creative development, design, engineering, production, and project management arm.

It creates and subsequently updates - from concept initiation through installation - all Disney resorts, theme parks and attractions, real estate developments, entertainment venues, and new media projects.

The Imagineering unit is Disney's main driver of innovation and profit.

Disney fuses timeless fables with futuristic technology into fascinating tableaus for family experiences and fun.

It's done it for 50+ years and likely will do so for another 50 years.

Imagination clearly is a timeless resource that creates real value out of neurons. It also is an inexhaustible resource that can create products of universal appeal.

Imagination may lay idle in many organizations, but those who spark it can create a profitable global business empire.

You don't have to be in the entertainment business to imagine "what will happen" after "what happens next" for your business.

QUESTIONS to ASK

- Am I (are we) imaginative enough?
- Do we need an "Imagineering" unit?
- What is the most imaginative future we can come up with for our organization?
- What else do we have to imagine in order to make it become a reality?

JUSTIFY

FUTURISTIC MEANING

To assess and evaluate the truth of things. To use proper evaluative judgment in pursuing goals. To act in a just, reasonable, and right manner. To prove or pronounce what is proper. To treat as righteous and just.

Similar to: Warrant, vindicate, justify, expose.

Opposites: Distort, confuse, obscure, cover up.

QUOTATIONS to INSPIRE YOU
to
JUSTIFY

Rule #1:
Use your good judgment in all situations.
(There will be no additional rules)
— *Nordstrom Employee Manual*

Better than the one who knows what is right is
he who loves what is right.
— *Confucius*

You cannot depend on your judgment
when your imagination is out of focus.
It isn't safe to sit in judgment upon another
person's illusion when you are not on the
inside. While you are thinking it is
a dream, he may know it is a planet.
— *Mark Twain (author)*

Experts often possess
more data than judgment.
— *Colin Powell (US Secretary of State)*

Reason and judgment are
the qualities of a leader.
— *Cornelius Tacitus (historian)*

FUTURISTIC LEADERSHIP PRINCIPLE

Judge the truth of the future, and act justly.

Use a moral compass that has a "true north" - a code of conduct which constantly steers judgment and future decisions in the proper direction.

EXAMPLE and APPLICATION

Futuristic leaders always practice a clear moral code. Their goals are always worthy, justified, and justifiable - not just achievable.

Thanks to his personal discipline and strength of character, George Washington was then, and still stands today, as the exemplar of just and effective leadership.

As a young boy, Washington wrote out 110 "Rules of Civility and Decent Behavior in Company and Conversation" and forever strived throughout his life to conduct himself by these rules.

At age 17, he started and mastered a business as a surveyor - a profession which early on established his reputation for thoroughness and high virtue.

After leading the colonies to victory, Washington spurned demands that he become "king," instead voluntarily resigning his commission and thus setting the precedent for civilian rule.

Washington set high ethical and moral standards and lived by them: personal discipline, integrity, and a leadership responsibility to set an example of impeccable character for those who succeeded him.

America's first President set a moral compass that, along with the Constitution, guides the nation's future.

If their moral compass goes awry, even the most-successful leaders can lose their bearings and steer their organizations way off course and into danger-ous predicaments if not total disaster.

Such executives surround themselves with "yes men" (note: most corporate whistle-blowers are women!) who are afraid to challenge questionable or unjustifiable decisions.

True leaders surround themselves with people of highest integrity. Always ready to be judged, they keep close counsel with a few trusted advisors who will challenge unjustified decisions.

They also know that if errors in judgment, which can befall anyone, go unimpeded, they will soon create a permissive culture that, in turn, can lead to criminal actions and fraud. Their moral compass prevents that and leads to success.

QUESTIONS to ASK

- How well-justified is our mission?
- What is our "true North" and how do we maintain it?
- How will others construe this decision?

KNOW

FUTURISTIC MEANING

To have clear, almost-certain perception. To have a belief or faith in something as true beyond any doubt - as that the sun will rise in the morning. To possess wisdom or information. To be cognizant or aware of; possess knowledge about. To know how, be familiar or acquainted with, or have first-hand knowledge of.

Similar to: Recognize, experience, tune-in.

Opposites: Ignore, tune-out.

QUOTATIONS to INSPIRE YOU
to
KNOW

**To be conscious that you are ignorant
is a great step towards knowledge.**
— *Benjamin Disraeli (UK Prime Minister)*

**The leader must know,
must know that he knows,
and make it abundantly clear to those around
him that he knows.**
— *Clarence B. Randall (Inland Steel Co)*

**If you have knowledge,
let others light their candles in it.**
— *Margaret Fuller (feminist)*

**O, that a man might know the end of
this day's business ere it come!**
— *William Shakespeare (playwright)*

**Knowledge will forever govern ignorance; and
people who mean to be their own governors
must arm themselves with
the power which knowledge gives.**
— *James Madison (4th US President)*

FUTURISTIC LEADERSHIP PRINCIPLE

Know yourself, and be all-knowing about the future and how to get there.

Self-knowledge creates purpose. Knowledge develops daily and can be leveraged. Know what you don't know, and get to know what you need.

EXAMPLE and APPLICATION

Pure "knowledge companies" grow based on brainpower, continuous learning and innovation.

Buckman Labs was started by a husband and wife team in 1945 in a small house in Memphis. Dr. Stanley Buckman and his wife Mertie had one product, a 50-gallon process vessel, and four staff. Today, Buckman is a global business making 500+ products in more than 70 countries.

Buckman had a unique ability to create and make innovative solutions to control the growth of micro-organisms. Today, it provides advanced chemical treatments and extensive technical services to resolve complex industrial problems.

Its specialty chemicals include microbicides, scale and corrosion inhibitors, polymers, dispersants, and defoamers for use in industries such as pulp and paper, water treatment, leather, coatings & plastics, wood, and agriculture.

Buckman regularly wins "knowledge management" awards and constantly records double digit growth.

Such futuristic knowledge leaders leverage the "knowledge multiplier effect." The faster and farther knowledge is moved and shared, the more it grows and the greater its value.

Leadership isn't always about having perfect knowledge but knowing when you have enough and how
to use it. In fact, it's often better to be approxi-
mately right than precisely wrong. How many holes-
in-one are there?

Indeed, if you know exactly and with precise
certainty how to reach your objective - unless
you're going to the Moon - you probably need to set
a more challenging goal.

QUESTIONS to ASK

- Who am I, at the deepest level?
- What do I most want?
- What else do I need to know?
- How knowledgeable is this organization?
- How much do we know about our future?
- How well do we leverage our know-how?

LEARN

FUTURISTIC MEANING

To acquire or gain knowledge or skills for the future. To commit to memory; learn by heart. To study a certain subject. To find out. To fix in the mind.

Similar to: Discover, ascertain, find out, apprehend.

Opposites: Misunderstand, clueless, miss the point.

QUOTATIONS to INSPIRE YOU
to
LEARN

**Formal education will make you a living.
Self-education will make you a fortune.**
— *Jim Rohn (motivational speaker)*

**Tell me, I'll forget.
Show me, I may remember,
But involve me, and I'll understand.**
— *Chinese Proverb*

**To attain knowledge, add things every day.
To attain wisdom, remove things every day.**
— *Lao Tsu (philosopher)*

**If I've seen farther than others, it's
because I stood on the shoulders of giants.**
— *Isaac Newton (scientist)*

**The illiterate of the future
will not be the person who cannot read.
It will be the person who
does not know how to learn.**
— *Alvin Toffler (futurist)*

FUTURISTIC LEADERSHIP PRINCIPLE

The more you learn, the greater your potential, the broader your future options.

Learning is about restructuring the meaning of your experience to make it more future relevant. Learning will transform and enrich you. Explore something new, and you will endow your future.

EXAMPLE and APPLICATION

Futuristic executives feed their brains, lest they wither and die. The most successful companies learn to adapt and constantly evolve. Those that do not learn to change, go extinct.

General Electric is the world's most successful "learning" company. Of the original Dow 100 stocks, only GE survives. Thanks to 100 years of accumulated brain power, it ranks #1 in the world.

GE constantly re-invents itself based on the future it sees. Its learning culture enables it to constantly evolve and adapt. Under Jack Welch, it explicitly defined itself as a learning company and it spends more than $1 billion a year on leadership training.

GE builds a strong cadre of future leaders by a relentless focus on nurturing leadership talent, growing people up a learning spiral from Emerging to Executive Leader.

This commitment to continuous learning gives GE its true competitive edge: the ability to propel itself forward and ensure another 100 years of success.

Learn something new every single day, and remember it. Also remember to forget something old every single day - clear your brain of outmoded ideas and knowledge.

Also learn from a neutral point of view. Don't have preconceived ideas and notions about what you need to know. Respond to situations with learning in mind, realize what you don't know, and set explicit learning objectives. Make a "to do" list of what you need to learn.

Encourage employees to do the same. Turn learning into a performance goal and ask your people to set learning goals as part of their annual review: "This year, I will learn about X so that I can do Y."

Refresh your learning daily, but you should do it in depth at least as often as you publish your financial statements. Then you'll have a "lifelong learning organization" in no time!

QUESTIONS to ASK

- How well do I learn?
- What should I learn next?
- How good a learning organization are we?
- What learning goals should we set?

MOTIVATE

FUTURISTIC MEANING

To provide with a motive to achieve a common goal. To give an incentive to. To induce.

Similar to: Enthuse, arouse, excite, inspire, ignite, spark, turn on.

Opposites: Dampen, dismay, douse, extinguish, paralyze, turn off.

QUOTATIONS to INSPIRE YOU
to
MOTIVATE

**Motivation is the art of getting people
to do what you want them to do
because they want to do it.**
— *Dwight Eisenhower (34th US President)*

**Motivate, train, care about, and
make winners out of them ... and
they'll treat the customers right.**
— *J. Marriott Jr. (Marriott Corp)*

**No one can develop anyone but himself.
That door locks on the inside.**
— *Chris Argyris (organization guru)*

**By changing inner attitudes, people can
change the outer aspects of their lives.**
— *William James (psychologist)*

**As for the best leaders, the people do not
notice their existence. When the best leader's
work is done, the people say,
"We did it ourselves!"**
— *Lao-Tsu (philosopher)*

FUTURISTIC LEADERSHIP PRINCIPLE

Persuade people to "buy in" to a future and they will be motivated to achieve it.

It's not about motivating people. People must motivate themselves. Relate what you are doing to their natural behavior - to their primary motivations and aspirations - and they will eagerly "buy in" and start moving.

EXAMPLE and APPLICATION

Motivation is a state of mind. It comes from inside. Futuristic leaders see what others can't see in themselves; they help them cultivate and draw out their own achievement abilities. They also gain inspiration from other great motivators.

Winston Churchill is head and shoulders above everybody for his ability to inspire, motivate, and embolden people to succeed.

On the night of 9/11, New York mayor Giuliani read a Churchill biography for inspiration on how to guide the city through the aftermath of tragedy.

Churchill displayed astonishing strength in leading the British people through the horrors of war and in energizing troops to victory. Without him, it is fair to say World War II would not have been won.

There will never be another Churchill. But of the many lessons we can learn from him are these:

- Nothing beats the persuasive passion of "blood-toil-tears-sweat";
- You need dogged determination to win;

- Protect your key people from meddling bureaucrats;
- Sustain high expectations and moral standards;
- Stay positive and enthusiastic, no matter what;
- Always lead by example, by "going to the front."

Motivational leaders don't need desks; they get "out front." They "walk the talk" and establish themselves as role models. Watching them, others try to raise their own standards to match. Such genuine leaders motivate merely by being highly admired for their vision, perseverance, and other futuristic leadership A-Z attributes.

Just by being a futuristic leader, your charisma and magnetism will stir others to motivate themselves to go with you into the future.

To further turn your people on, help them to identify their own primary motivating factor and how it will be satisfied by collective goals.

QUESTIONS to ASK

- What motivates me and my team?
- What is our primary motivating factor?
- What will get them jumping out of bed early every morning?

NAVIGATE

FUTURISTIC MEANING

To guide and steer to a new place.
To act as the navigator. To direct a course of travel. To chose and pursue the best path.

Similar to: Pilot, pioneer, helm, maneuver, trailblaze.

Opposites: Go around in circles, get lost, run aground, sink.

QUOTATIONS to INSPIRE YOU
to
NAVIGATE

**Don't be afraid to take big steps.
You can't cross a chasm
in two small jumps.**
— David Lloyd George (UK Prime Minister)

**Following the light of the sun,
we left the Old World.**
— Christopher Columbus (explorer)

**Leadership is going where
nobody else has gone.**
— Robert Galvin (Motorola)

**If you don't change direction,
you'll end up where you're headed.**
— Chinese proverb

**The real art of discovery consists
not in finding new lands
but in seeing with new eyes.**
— Marcel Proust (novelist)

FUTURISTIC LEADERSHIP PRINCIPLE

Leadership in a networked world is about light-speed navigation across a broad and unexplored digital domain.

Navigators transplant themselves into the future, scout the future constantly for the next options, and show others how to achieve them.

EXAMPLE and APPLICATION

Leaders must venture into the digital economy. That demands fearless courage and the skill to navigate with no "map" but that in their minds.

Jeff Bezos, founder of Amazon.com and the first billionaire of e-commerce, has become a legend in his own time.

In 1994, Bezos quit a $1-million-a-year job at a New York hedge fund and headed across the continent to launch not only the world's biggest bookstore but a path-breaking online general merchandiser that is "Wal-Marting the Web."

He and his wife flew to Dallas; then she drove from there to Seattle while he typed Amazon's business plan on a laptop and phoned investors. Upon arrival, he began shipping books out of his garage.

Defying skeptics, Bezos saw how retailing would shift online and that personalized and customized service, value prices, and overnight delivery would be the future of shopping. And he's proving it.

Bezos often relates how his passion to be a pioneer in a brand new industry sustained him. Super-smart, and ever-irrepressible, Bezos maintains that this is just the beginning. He says Amazon's website is "stone-age" compared

67

with what it will become and that companies which successfully navigate the future of online consumer satisfaction will dominate.

As Amazon showed, when you navigate the future, obstacles are challenges to be overcome. Amazon was a toddler that was off and running from the get go.

In life, toddlers are motivated to walk, discover a brand new world, and broaden their horizons. They wobble, stumble, bump into things, and fall. But they pick themselves up, keep going, and learn fast.

Amazon never stumbled once. So start toddling! You'll soon run. Like Amazon, take a new path, not the worn trail. A vision is the first step on the journey. Map it with detailed, intentional steps, and definitive directions. Grab your compass and take your people into the future.

QUESTIONS to ASK

- How good a navigator am I?
- How well does our organization navigate its path?
- What's our guiding star? How will we adjust our course?
- What might throw us off course? How then will we course correct?

ORGANIZE

FUTURISTIC MEANING

To plan and direct a complex undertaking.
To create or form a group or organization to achieve an objective. To systematically plan a united effort.

Similar to: Mastermind, arrange, coordinate, put together, codify, formulate, get going.

Opposites: Disorganize, confuse, derange, fragment, disperse, disband.

QUOTATIONS to INSPIRE YOU
to
ORGANIZE

Don't agonize, organize.
— *Florynce R. Kennedy (activist)*

**It isn't the incompetent who destroy
an organization. It's those who want
to rest on their achievements who
are forever clogging things up.**
— *Charles Sorenson (law professor)*

**To build a ship, don't herd people together
to collect wood and don't assign them
tasks and work. Teach them to long
for the endless immensity of the sea.**
— *Antoine de Saint-Exupery (pilot, poet)*

**Progress is to preserve order amid change,
and to preserve change amid order.**
— *Alfred North Whitehead (mathematician)*

**Organization man is dead.
He thrived in smokestack America.
When computers were huge and
an apple was something you ate.**
— *Bruce Nussbaum ("Business Week")*

FUTURISTIC LEADERSHIP PRINCIPLE

Organize diffuse energy and shape it into an overwhelming force to achieve goals.

Organize and prioritize. And be good at multi-tasking so that you can organize things even in the most chaotic of circumstances.

EXAMPLE and APPLICATION

When you think of superb organizations, the names that come to mind are courier companies such as FedEx or fast-food companies such as McDonald's - companies which organize a massive array of activities to serve individual customer needs, quickly and efficiently. But there are other unsung exemplar organizers, and this one may surprise you.

Within 23 minutes of the Oklahoma bombing, three canteens were on the scene, provided by the Salvation Army - a global organization serving 30 million people on a $2 billion budget.

Called "the most effective organization" in the U.S. by Peter Drucker, the Army follows eight principles:

1. A purpose that transcends quarterly earnings;
2. Serving human needs;
3. Publicly accountable to visible standards;
4. Encourage feedback and act upon it;
5. Invest real responsibility in top people;
6. Accept the inevitability of change;
7. Take calculated risks; and
8. Motivate employees by ensuring their jobs are both valuable and enjoyable.

The Army says the key is to "organize to improvise" - not surprising when you consider the array of its services:

71

alcohol, drug, and prisoner rehab; homeless shelters; disaster relief and rebuilding; etc. Its mission is based on the gospel's injunction to teach and to serve - two timeless aspects of leadership - through holistic solutions.

Leadership is essentially holistic because, of course, organizations are organic organisms, constantly evolving in an environment that is in a state of flux.

The key is to marshal and orchestrate the deployment of resources and teams such that they can respond instantly and effectively to changed demands.

QUESTIONS to ASK

- How well organized am I?
- How suitably organized is our organization?
- Are we organized to improvise?
- How well do we focus our energy?

PERSEVERE

FUTURISTIC MEANING

To persist in any business or enterprise under-taken. To pursue steadily any project or course begun. To maintain a purpose in spite of counter influence, opposition or discouragement.

Similar to: Hang in, endure, keep going, press on; Be sure-footed, steadfast, tenacious, unfazed, unwavering.

Opposites: Abandon, hesitate, falter, throw in the towel.

QUOTATIONS to INSPIRE YOU
to
PERSEVERE

You've got to say,
"I think that if I keep working at this,
and want it bad enough, I can have it."
It's called perseverance.
— *Lee Iacocca (Chrysler Corp)*

It is not the mountain we conquer
but ourselves.
— *Edmund Hillary (mountaineer)*

But I have promises to keep,
And miles to go before I sleep.
— *Robert Frost (poet)*

Successful people keep moving.
They make mistakes, but they don't quit.
— *Conrad Hilton (Hilton Hotels)*

Success is the ability to
go from failure to failure
without losing your enthusiasm.
— *Winston S. Churchill (UK Prime Minister)*

FUTURISTIC LEADERSHIP PRINCIPLE

Take small steps but keep driving towards the big long-term objective.

The smaller your step, the easier the climb to the highest peak. Be determined not to give up. Failure is the path of least persistence.

EXAMPLE and APPLICATION

Perseverance requires self-discipline. For your organi-zation to reach its destination, you must take the first steps yourself. But major gains are rarely achieved in one leap, but step-by-step.

Abraham Lincoln was one of our greatest leaders. But there were many set-backs and incremental improve-ments in his life:

Age 1: Born into poverty	Age 2: Infant brother died
Age 7: Almost drowned	Age 9: Mother died
Age 10: Nearly killed by horse	Age 16: Took a job
Age 19: Sister died	Age 23: Lost his job
Age 23: Lost run for office	Age 24: Failed in business
Age 25: Elected to state office	Age 26: Sweetheart died
Age 27: Re-elected	Age 28: Nervous breakdown
Age 29: Lost for Speaker	Age 29: Re-elected
Age 31: Re-elected	Age 31: Filed for bankruptcy
Age 34: Lost for Congress	Age 39: Lost re-nomination
Age 40: Lost for land office	Age 41: Son died
Age 42: Father died	Age 45: Lost Senate race
Age 47: Lost for Vice-Pres	Age 49: Lost Senate race
Age 52: Elected President	Age 56: Re-elected President

In 1863, loath to leave his desk and family, and not well, he agreed to "say a few words" in Gettysburg. In 272 words, spoken in 2 minutes, he literally re-made America and secured its democratic freedom.

There are only experiences, never failures. Each life step, forward or back, prepares us for the next step, and finally for the last big stride, moving us towards our destiny. So far, Lincoln's 272 words have galvanized American society for 140 years. And they will keep on doing so.

Such tenacity and precise purposefulness will always endure. If you ever feel you want to stop, keep going another few minutes. Resist the temptations to take a break, other than for a much-needed rest. Write one more e-mail, make one more phone call, strike another item off the "to do" list. Write 272 words of destiny.

Embed perseverance as part of your leadership style. You will surprise and surpass yourself, and you could inspire generations of others.

Of course, persistence does not mean the blind pursuit of a wrong path or exhausting yourself. You must reassess and change course as needed to achieve a still-valid goal. But always press on down that chosen revised path.

QUESTIONS to ASK

- How persistent is our organization?
- What step will move us toward our goal?
- What lasting miracle could I achieve with a 2 minute speech?

QUESTION

FUTURISTIC MEANING

To challenge and examine the accuracy, probity, propriety and true progress of a desired outcome. To investigate and probe. To discuss and debate, without "begging the question" as to the point in question.

Similar to: Ask about, challenge, go over, sound out.

Opposites: Accept at face value.

QUOTATIONS to INSPIRE YOU
to
QUESTION

**Asking questions is the A-B-C of diagnosis.
Only the inquiring mind solves problems.**
— *Edward Hodnett (writer)*

**He who asks is a fool for a minute.
He who does not, remains a fool forever.**
— *Chinese Proverb*

He that questioneth much, shall learn much.
— *Francis Bacon (deductive philosopher)*

**A major stimulant to creative thinking is
focused questions. There is something about a
well-worded question that often penetrates to
the heart of the matter
and triggers new ideas and insights.**
— *Brian Tracy (motivational author)*

**The wise man doesn't
give the right answers;
he poses the right questions.**
— *Claude Levi-Strauss (structuralist)*

FUTURISTIC LEADERSHIP PRINCIPLE

Probe your objectives to stay on course.

Question and listen for clues to better meet stake-
holder expectations. And always focus more on
what's working than what is not.

EXAMPLE and APPLICATION

Futuristic leaders ask questions that lead to new
ideas, improved products, and better decisions.

> **Michael Dell asked, "Why can't people buy computers
> directly?" So he conceived of Dell Computer in his
> college dorm and proceeded to build it into the
> world's #1 PC maker.**
>
> He uses questions to avoid internal "group think" and to
> help identify external customer needs. "Group think" traps
> you by approaching problems too similarly. To encourage
> innovative thinking, Dell words questions from various
> perspectives, on all aspects of the business. To inject
> improvement and innovation into Dell's culture, he teaches
> people to approach a problem or opportunity holistically.
>
> Dell also asks customers, "What do you really want this to
> do; what's another way to achieve that?" and asks suppli-
> ers, "Can we do this differently?" Then they look for a
> totally new approach that exceeds original objectives and
> customer expectations.
>
> To further tap outside info, Michael Dell uses novel
> approaches to learn what people think of Dell. He anony-
> mously hangs out in chat rooms where users talk about
> products and their likes and dislikes.

Good questions are a good way to find out where
you stand and where you intend to end up. They

79

reveal what's important and focus people's attention and efforts on that.

Strategic questions focus on what is working well and how to improve further. They invite eager participation in new options.

By contrast, questions which focus on what's not working are adversarial and accusatory. They make people clam up, deplete creativity, and entrench resistance to change.

Afraid to reveal mistakes or weakness, people hide behind outmoded rules and processes. Afraid to err, they make still more errors. They also focus more on "What's in it for me?" rather than seeking new organization-wide options.

Asking the right questions thus sets a strategic mindset by identifying what's truly working, and why. That spurs thoughts about what might be even more ideal, what lessons are transferable to other efforts, and what new resources are needed.

QUESTIONS to ASK

- How well do we question ourselves?
- What are the right questions to accomplish this?
- How can I best word it?
- What are the answers telling us?

RESPOND

FUTURISTIC MEANING

To respond to what needs to be done.
To react to, to render satisfaction, to answer and be responsible for. To promise to support [from the Latin *responsum* ("to promise") and an architectural "pillar supporting an arch"].

Similar to: Accept, answer, reply, rejoin, bolster.

Opposites: Abdicate, disregard, ignore, avoid, overlook, pass over, reject, snub.

QUOTATIONS to INSPIRE YOU
to
RESPOND

**You cannot escape the responsibility
of tomorrow, by evading it today.**
— *Abraham Lincoln (16th US President)*

The price of greatness is responsibility.
— *Winston S. Churchill (UK Prime Minister)*

**We are not here merely to make a living.
We are here to enrich the world.**
— *Woodrow Wilson (18th US President)*

**When you point a finger at someone else,
remember that four of your fingers
are pointing at yourself.**
— *Louis Nizer (lawyer)*

**You must take personal responsibility.
You cannot change the circumstances,
the seasons, or the wind,
but you can change yourself.
That is something you have charge of.**
— *Jim Rohn (motivational speaker)*

FUTURISTIC LEADERSHIP PRINCIPLE

Responsibility is the ability to respond, or "response-ability." It starts by responding to what the future offers and demands.

You cannot change external circumstances. But you must take primary responsibility, and respond to changing customer needs and business conditions.

EXAMPLE and APPLICATION

Responsible companies put their customers first and their shareholders last. If the customer is satisfied, so will be the shareholder.

Johnson & Johnson, formed in 1896 by three brothers to make antiseptic bandages, is the world's most comprehensive maker of health care products. J&J operates 200 companies in 57 countries, sells products in 175 countries, and employs 110,000 worldwide. J&J has no mission statement but rather this unique "Credo" that has guided its operations since 1943:

Our first responsibility is to the doctors, nurses and patients, to mothers and fathers, and all others who use our products and services.
In meeting their needs everything we do must be of high quality. Orders must be serviced promptly and accurately.

We are responsible to all our employees worldwide.
Everyone must be considered as an individual. We must respect their dignity and recognize their merit. They must have a sense of security in their jobs. Compensation must be fair and adequate, and working conditions clean, orderly and safe. We must be mindful of ways to help our employees fulfill their family responsibilities. Employees must feel free to make suggestions and complaints. There must be equal opportunity for employment, development

and advancement for those qualified. We must provide competent management,
and their actions must be just and ethical.

We are responsible to the communities in which we live and work, and to the world community as well.
We must be good citizens - support good works and charities and bear our fair share of taxes. We must encourage civic improvements and better health and education. We must maintain in good order the property we are privileged to use, protecting the environment and natural resources.

Our final responsibility is to our stockholders.
Business must make a sound profit. We must experiment with new ideas. Research must be carried on, innovative programs developed and mistakes paid for. New equipment must be purchased, new facilities provided and new products launched.
Reserves must be created to provide for adverse times. When we operate according to these principles, the stockholders should realize a fair return.

No wonder J&J's sales growth, profit, and ROI routinely outstrip those of competitors. J&J always responds in a responsible way.

QUESTIONS to ASK

- How responsive am I to our clients?
- How responsive is our culture?
- Do we have our priorities right?

STRATEGIZE

FUTURISTIC MEANING

To make important considerations relating to, or concerned with, a grand strategy or plan of action.
To synthesize options and opportunities and then organize to obtain them.

Similar to: Aim, blueprint, design, "modus operandi".

Opposites: Aimless, meander, move in "ad hoc" fashion.

QUOTATIONS to INSPIRE YOU
to
STRATEGIZE

There is a tide in the affairs of men,
which, taken at the flood,
leads to fortune.
— *William Shakespeare (playwright)*

A good goal is like a strenuous exercise
- it makes you stretch.
— *Mary Kay Ash (Mary Kay)*

Only those who will risk going too far
can possibly find out how far one can go.
— *T.S. Eliot (poet, playwright)*

Strategy without tactics
is the slowest route to victory.
Tactics without strategy
is the noise before defeat.
— *Sun Tzu (strategist)*

It doesn't matter whether the cat is
black or white so long as it catches mice.
Socialism is not poverty;
It is glorious to get rich.
— *Deng Xiaoping (Chinese Leader)*

FUTURISTIC LEADERSHIP PRINCIPLE

Strategic goals make previously-impossible objectives now achievable.

No matter what the current situation, you will achieve what you set out to do, if you properly assess the situation and lay out proper plans.

EXAMPLE and APPLICATION

Strategic intention stretches you toward your goal. But dramatic change often demands a clean break from past ways of doing things.

The best-articulated and most-well executed "clean-break" strategy of the 20th century is that of China, under market reformer, Deng Xiaoping.

Dismissed three times by Mao, but always brought back as "indispensable," when Deng finally gained supreme power, he asked think tanks for a "SWOT" analysis (strengths, weaknesses, opportunities, and threats) and a study of trends (social, technical, economic, and political) impacting China.

Based on their findings, in 1978 Deng launched a sweeping "4 Modernizations" program and set a humungous goal for China, not only to quadruple its economy from 1980 to 2000 but to catch up with the mid-income countries by 2050.

The year 2000 goal was achieved by 1996, at the fastest pace of any country in history. Still growing rapidly, the new goal is to double again by 2010, to create a "well-off society." The goals for 2050 remain in place, but long before then China will be the world's #1 economy.

China's astonishing economic performance sets an example for all of us. Whether you are a fledgling entrepreneur in capitalist America, or a formerly-closed Stalinist totalitarian state, you can achieve economic miracles within a relatively short period of time.

Successful business enterprises need to focus on each business unit and make three simple assessments:

1. What is our "global" competitive environment and how is it changing?
2. What are our main competitors doing?
3. What's our plan to leapfrog over them?

Do a proper "SWOT" analysis and evaluation of the 4-STEP trends you face, then develop a responsive strategy and tactics, and you will achieve remarkable progress.

QUESTIONS to ASK

- How strategic am I?
- How strategic is our organization? Do we think big enough?
- Which goal, when achieved, will have the greatest positive effect?
- How could we quadruple our net income, over what time period?

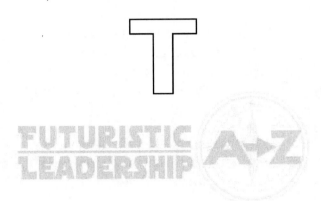

TEACH

FUTURISTIC MEANING

To impressively impart future-relevant skills or knowledge to others.
To introduce and accustom gradually to some new knowledge, action, rules, or attitude.
To guide and mentor. To show how.

Similar to: Counsel, coach, instruct, inform, inculcate, show-n-tell.

Opposites: Ignore, leave to founder, confuse, dumbfound.

QUOTATIONS to INSPIRE YOU
to
TEACH

The teacher is one who
makes two ideas grow
where only one grew before.
— *Elbert Hubbard (writer, publisher)*

Teachers open the door,
but you must enter by yourself.
— *Chinese proverb*

I talk in order to understand;
I teach in order to learn.
— *Robert Frost (poet)*

Better than 1,000 days of diligent study,
is one day with a great teacher.
— *Japanese proverb*

The mediocre teacher tells.
The good teacher explains.
The superior teacher demonstrates.
The great teacher inspires.
— *William Arthur Ward (pastor, teacher)*

FUTURISTIC LEADERSHIP PRINCIPLE

Teach that which supports your goals; eliminate what hinders your progress.

Raise people to a new level of future-relevant understanding. Widen people's viewpoints so they can grow. Mentor them towards their own success - and to be your successors.

EXAMPLE and APPLICATION

Mentor was a loyal advisor to Odysseus, in Homer's *Odyssey*, who entrusted him with the care and education of his son. To "mentor" someone thus means to responsibly advise, teach, and coach them.

The world's greatest business teacher and mentor is Peter Drucker - the North Star of responsible business leadership ideas.

The prolific author of scores of business books and articles, he has a unique way of seeing the big picture and helping people see their role within it.

Drucker also understands what many executives do not: have faith in people, building on their strengths to make any weaknesses irrelevant. Learn what interests them, and help them build their strengths around that.

Drucker calls himself a "social ecologist" who's always thinking about how things fit together. Now in his mid-90s, he draws on a rich knowledge base to fill his advice with examples and analogies, all synthesized into sage but actionable decisions.

A mentor's greatest gift is to say, "You can do it!" and to show how. Mentors teach "how" to do something, not "what" to do. Mentors help sharpen other people's skills and visions.

True mentors have huge and lasting influence - the true measure of leadership. You cannot mentor unless you can lead. And you cannot lead unless you too have at least one mentor.

That said, we tend to "become" more than 50% of the models we choose to be influenced by. The key is to emulate not imitate, by remaining true to yourself.

QUESTIONS to ASK

- Who should be my own mentors?
- How can I improve as a mentor?
- How well does our organization mentor?
- With whom should I share the knowledge I have gained over the past year?
- With whom should they share their knowledge and experience?

UPLIFT

FUTURISTIC MEANING

To fill with high spirits and optimism, and raise to a higher elevation. To raise aloft.

Similar to: Upthrust, elate, elevate, pick up, boost, buck up, buoy, embolden, exhilarate, inspire, invigorate, gladden, hearten, perk up, turn on.

Opposites: Bring down, depress, dismay, dishearten, turn off.

QUOTATIONS to INSPIRE YOU
to
UPLIFT

**If you want to lift yourself up,
lift someone else.**
— *Booker T. Washington ("Up From Slavery")*

**Leadership is lifting a person's vision
to higher sights, the raising of a person's
performance to a higher standard.**
— *Peter F. Drucker (management guru)*

**Look forward, do not look backward.
Gather afresh in heart and spirit all the
energies of your being. Bend anew together
for a supreme effort.**
— *Winston S. Churchill (UK Prime Minister)*

**Treat a man as if he were already
what he potentially could be,
and you make him what he should be.**
— *Johann Wolfgang von Goethe (playwright)*

**To achieve a high "C" I imagine myself to be a
show-jumping horse, approaching a very high
fence, then soaring over it.**
— *Luciano Pavarotti (opera superstar)*

FUTURISTIC LEADERSHIP PRINCIPLE

To progress, practice uplifting praise.

Give yourself and your team a boosting pep talk. As you rise, others will help you go higher still. Together you will soar.

EXAMPLE and APPLICATION

When dark clouds gather, people sometimes need help to see beyond them. They need lifting up and inspiring to see a brighter future ahead.

John F. Kennedy kicked off his presidency with an inspiring inaugural address, only 19 minutes long, that uplifted an entire nation.

At the height of the Cold War, Kennedy inspired America to embrace change, accept individual and national responsibility, and move forward into the second-half of the 20th century.

His call to duty still rings true today and his words can be used to inspire any organizational effort, as these few timeless extracts convey:

We observe today a celebration of freedom - symbolizing an end as well as a beginning - signifying renewal as well as change. Let the word go forth from this time and place, to friend and foe alike, that the torch has been passed to a new generation of Americans.

United, there is little we cannot do in a host of cooperative ventures. So let us begin anew. Let's explore what problems unite us instead of belaboring those problems which divide us. Together let us explore the stars, conquer the deserts, eradicate disease, tap the ocean depths, and encourage the arts and commerce.

In your hands, my fellow citizens, more than in mine, will rest the final success or failure of our course. Since this country was founded, each generation of Americans has been summoned to give testimony to its national loyalty.

Now the trumpet summons us again. In the long history of the world, only a few generations have been granted the role of defending freedom in its hour of maximum danger. I do not shrink from this responsibility - I welcome it. I do not believe that any of us would exchange places with any other people or any other generation. The energy, the faith, the devotion which we bring to this endeavor will light our country and all who serve it - and the glow from that fire can truly light the world.

And so, my fellow Americans: ask not what your country can do for you - ask what you can do for your country. My fellow citizens of the world: ask not what America will do for you, but what together we can do for the freedom of man.

Major projects need a big lift at the start and lots of energy until they run smoothly. Airplanes use maximum fuel to get airborne but cruise with 63% less fuel. A flock of geese flies 72% faster than a lone goose. People are the same once they start cruising, especially in teams.

While change creates uncertainty you must raise people above it, so that divisions dissolve and the entire organization's future can be seen more clearly and achieved more easily.

QUESTIONS to ASK

- How can I be more uplifting?
- How good are we at taking off and soaring to a cruising altitude?

VISUALIZE

FUTURISTIC MEANING

To imagine, conceive of, see a large vision in one's mind. To make visual, or visible to others. To form a mental image of something not present before the eye at the time.

Similar to: Envision, project, picture, anticipate, foresee.

Opposites: Blind, unseeing, oblivious.

QUOTATIONS to INSPIRE YOU
to
VISUALIZE

**Large views always triumph
over small ideas.
It is better to have an ambitious
plan that none at all.**
— *Winston S. Churchill (UK Prime Minister)*

**Vision without action is a daydream.
Action without vision is a nightmare.**
— *Japanese proverb*

**A man that does not see visions
will never realize any high hope or
undertake any high enterprise.**
— *Woodrow Wilson (28th US President)*

**We want every person in the world
to taste Coca-Cola.**
— *Robert Woodruff (Coca Cola Co.)*

I see a computer on every desk.
— *Bill Gates (Microsoft)*

FUTURISTIC LEADERSHIP PRINCIPLE

The clearer, brighter, and simpler you visualize and describe your vision, the more it will magnetically pull others to it.

Visualization is the art of seeing the invisible. Place no limits on your vision. Visualization overcomes perceived limits. Visualize changes as being successful.

EXAMPLE and APPLICATION

Futuristic leaders have bifocal vision; they constantly switch back and forth between what's near at hand and in the far distance. Vision draws the leader to a clear target.

> **Bill Gates, co-founder and head of Microsoft, became the world's wealthiest person by envisioning a computer on every desk and then setting out to be the main supplier of software to those and similar devices.**
>
> Gates saw "a computer on every desk" at the very same time as established computer industry leaders said they could never see the day when anybody would ever need a computer at home.
>
> Gates constantly visualizes further developments in the computer and related industry and then steers his company toward opportunities he sees flowing from those changes.

Vision comes from asking two simple questions:
- Where is the world going?
- What do we do to capitalize on that?

To answer those questions, stand amid the future you preliminarily envision, experience and explore it, crystallize it into mental pictures, and map out how to get there.

If your vision doesn't capture the imagination of others, it's probably too small. Go back to the future and re-visualize it. Once it grabs people, use scenarios of the vision to rehearse your future.

Then design detailed plans about how to take advantage of what you visualize, based on your present situation and strengths versus those of potential competitors.

Futuristic leaders see all the twists and turns ahead. They see around corners well before other people even see the corner. How good is your x-ray vision?

QUESTIONS to ASK

- How well do I visualize, capture and articulate a vision?
- What vision will most captivate our organization, and our customers?
- In the simplest terms, what is our vision?

WEBIFY

FUTURISTIC MEANING

To "webolutionize" yourself and your organization, in parallel with the Internet revolution.

To change radically and completely. To fill with revolutionary ideas and overthrow old ways.

Similar to: Overturn, overthrow, remake, re-invent.

Opposites: Resist, rebel, mutiny, batten down the hatches.

QUOTATIONS to INSPIRE YOU
to
WEBIFY

Every generation needs a new revolution.
— *Thomas Jefferson (3rd US President)*

Any sufficiently advanced technology is indistinguishable from magic.
— *Arthur C. Clarke (space futurist)*

The Internet is totally transformational. It's the biggest thing that ever occurred in business in my lifetime.
— *Jack Welch (General Electric)*

Any company which does not become an e-business will not be in business.
— *Andy Grove (Intel)*

Virtually everything that was discussed about the Internet - even the most hyped thing - will happen. It just takes more time.
— *Bill Gates, in 2003 (Microsoft)*

FUTURISTIC LEADERSHIP PRINCIPLE

To succeed in the 21st century, you will either "webify" your business or die.

Technological revolutions never go backwards. Once invented, technology can't be un-invented. You have no choice but to re-invent your organization in parallel with the "webolution."

EXAMPLE and APPLICATION

Futuristic leaders view the future through the socio-economic network infostructure wrought by the Internet revolution, or "webolution." Because the Internet reconfigures the "value chain" into a "value web," they "webify" their companies, internally and externally.

> **Cisco Systems is not only a leading "value web" company, it supplies most of the routers which let the Internet function as a web.**
>
> Cisco "webified" its value chain to rely instead on a host of third party manufacturers, all connected via the Web. It operates as a virtual company over the Internet platform. As a result, two-thirds of the people who work for Cisco are not employed by it. Its entire product line is developed, built, delivered and installed by Web-linked partners.
>
> While Dell is the epitome of producer-to-consumer product fulfillment, Cisco is the leading business-to-business product fulfillment company. Their "value web" creates node-to-node, end-to-end visibility from the first front-office customer interaction to the last back-office transaction.

Before the Internet, companies needed huge back-office functions and manufacturing plants to service their operations. With the Internet, back-office functions get digitized and plants get robotized and/or outsourced to third parties, usually in low-wage countries.

There can be no doubting the "webolution": more than 700 million people worldwide now use the Web and 400 million shop online. In this digital global economy, companies simply have no choice but to be digitally competitive.

Companies which "webify" themselves to lead in e-commerce and become e-businesses will lead the way.

QUESTIONS to ASK

- How "webpreneurial" am I?
- How web-savvy is our Organization?
- What do we need to do to "webify" and become digitally competitive?

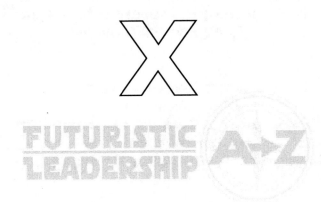

XEROGRAPH

FUTURISTIC MEANING

To clone or duplicate yourself. To form an image of futuristic leadership and proliferate it across the organization. To arrange an orderly succession to a next-generation leader.

Similar to: Copy, reproduce, multiply, evolve genetically.

Opposites: Pass on, die out.

QUOTATIONS to INSPIRE YOU
to
XEROX

**One person with passion is better
than 40 people merely interested.**
— *E. M. Forster (novelist)*

**If you want 1 year of prosperity,
grow corn.
If you want 10 years of prosperity,
grow trees.
If you want 100 years of prosperity,
grow people.**
— *Chinese Proverb*

**A leader's lasting value
is measured by succession.**
— *John C. Maxwell (motivational author)*

**Xerox does it again, and again,
and again and again, and ...**
— *Anonymous*

**I would rather make 1%
on the efforts of 100 people
than 100% on my own efforts.**
— *John Paul Getty (Getty Oil Corp)*

FUTURISTIC LEADERSHIP PRINCIPLE

Success without a successor is failure.

Leaders only create a legacy when they put their organization in a position to succeed without them. Futuristic leaders don't want followers but many more future leaders.

EXAMPLE and APPLICATION

Consciously or not, leaders reproduce themselves, warts and all. People copy the behavior they see. Futuristic leaders consciously and deliberately try to duplicate their behavior in others by growing them into leadership.

The best examples of executive duplication are store franchising (led by the familiar McDonald's) and network marketing. The latter is growing rapidly in parallel with the networked economy.

By far the leading network marketing company is Quixtar Corporation, launched online in 1999.

Growing faster than Amazon.com in its early years, Quixtar reached $1 billion in sales for 2003 and brought its cumulative 4-year bonus payout to its networked distributors to $1 billion.

A volume leader in its product categories, Quixtar grows by word-of-mouth and word-of-modem among online shoppers. Products are delivered direct to the home so that distributors don't worry about products but focus on personal relationships with shoppers.

Other e-commerce companies cannot match this unique "high-tech, high-touch" model. This model kept Quixtar growing through the dot-com shake-out of 2000-2001 and 9/11, from which it emerged stronger than ever.

. In essence, Quixtar can be seen as "individual franchising" where new entrants duplicate their mentors. They duplicate their leadership style, their successful business-building approaches, and that compounds sales growth.

All strategies are reproducible. Futuristic leaders put frameworks in place to ensure winning methods can be "Xeroxed" - duplicated and learned in an endless cycle of success.

We will see many more such strategies as the Internet revolution spreads and other consumer product companies learn "high-tech, high-touch" marketing from the likes of Quixtar.

QUESTIONS to ASK

- How reproducible am I?
- How well does our organization "xerox" itself?
- Can we be "high-tech, high-touch"?
- Can we switch to network marketing?

YIELD

FUTURISTIC MEANING

To lead and inspire by leveraging growth. To be flexible, bend like bamboo to achieve results. To sow seeds and harvest results, year in, year out.

Similar to: Render, return, generate, bring forth.

Opposites: Abandon, abdicate, admit defeat, fold.

QUOTATIONS to INSPIRE YOU
to
YIELD

**Pick the right people, give them the
opportunity to spread their wings,
and you don't have to manage them.**
— *Jack Welch (General Electric)*

**Hire people who are better than you are.
Then leave them to get on with it.**
— *David Ogilvy (Ogilvy & Mather)*

**Industry, perseverance, and frugality
make fortune yield.**
— *Benjamin Franklin (inventor)*

**Give me a place to stand,
a lever long enough,
and a fulcrum on which to place it,
and I will move the earth.**
— *Archimedes (inventor, engineer)*

**In business, the rearview mirror is
always clearer than the windshield.
Only buy what you're perfectly happy to
hold if the market shuts down for 10 years.**
— *Warren Buffett (Berkshire Hathaway)*

FUTURISTIC LEADERSHIP PRINCIPLE

Know and do that which yields high returns.

Leverage and multiply your human and other resources by continually investing in the future, compounding your assets to yield inevitable and enviable growth. Every step will pay a dividend.

EXAMPLE and APPLICATION

Jack up your car to change a wheel and you lift 2 tons - at least 20 times your own weight. Leverage your best minds and most productive projects, and you'll achieve the best results.

> **All wealth comes from the human mind, from ideas. But the best mind ever at creating pure wealth belongs to Warren Buffett, the head of Berkshire Hathaway.**
>
> Berkshire is a major holding company, with big stakes in many industries. Buffett uses the "value investing" strategy (of his mentor, Ben Graham) based on asset value, earnings power, and growth. To this, Buffett adds "franchise value" and focuses on the difference between price and value.
>
> Buffett admits missing $10 billion opportunities, yet Berkshire's average annual compound rate of return over 39 years is 22.2% versus 11% in the market as a whole. He has built a huge "franchise value" - and many millionaire shareholders.

When Buffett buys a company he leaves existing people in place and lets them run it. He buys underpriced (and often neglected) assets and then guides and helps his CEOs to leverage them to a realistic value. He injects capital and fresh-air common-sense thinking that breathes new life into the businesses, boosting their asset value.

To boost asset value requires that you raise the value of the brand or business franchise. These are best leveraged by investing in intellectual capital (people) and digital capital (Web-based knowledge), and by focusing on priority goals.

Focus on the top 20% of your people and the top 20% of your priority projects and, on average, that will yield 80% of your profits. That's a four-fold return on investment compared with spreading your focus too thinly.

Nourish all your best assets and you will reap rich future harvests.

QUESTIONS to ASK

- How can I better focus on the highest-yielding projects and people?
- How well does our organization identify and focus on those?
- How could we achieve a return which is twice that of the industry average?

ZOOM

FUTURISTIC MEANING

To grasp new opportunities and produce rapid results before others. To zoom-out to see the bigger picture. To zoom-in on the detail of what matters. To streak ahead and outpace others.

Similar to: Soar, buzz, dart, dash, scoot, outstrip, leapfrog, skyrocket, surge, zap, zip along.

Opposites: Fail to start, sputter, stall, go nowhere.

QUOTATIONS to INSPIRE YOU
to
ZOOM

**There comes a moment when
you have to stop revving the car
and shove it in gear.**
— *David J. Mahoney (Dana Foundation)*

**Things may come to those who wait,
but only things left by those who hustle.**
— *Abraham Lincoln (16th US President)*

The speed of the boss is the team's speed.
— *Lee Iococca (Chrysler Corp)*

**Move like a light beam,
Fly like lightning, Strike like thunder**.
— *Morihei Ueshiba (martial artist)*

**Going digital will put you on the leading edge
of a shock wave of change that will shatter the
old way of doing business.
A digital nervous system will let you do
"business at the speed of thought"
- the key to success in the 21st century.**
— *Bill Gates (Microsoft)*

FUTURISTIC LEADERSHIP PRINCIPLE

The future belongs to those who get there first - to those who move at digital speed.

Electrify all processes and operate in real-time, 24-hours a day, globally. Surprise, astonish, and delight your customers with your speed of service.

EXAMPLE and APPLICATION

The telephone led to the fax machine and the Internet brought e-mail, speeding up business cycle times. Customers raised with remote controls, banking machines, and cellphones simply expect fast service. Such trends force many changes, especially new ways of business.

Speed is in Fred Smith's genes. His grandfather captained paddle steamers, his father founded Greyhound, and he's a licensed pilot. Naturally, then, in 1971 he founded FedEx and swiftly changed the world of delivery.

In 1971, the year the microchip was invented, Smith foresaw today's fast-cycle economy and became obsessed with time, speed, and reliability. FedEx leapfrogged its competitors and today does a remarkable $23 billion a year in business.

That's because FedEx digitized everything to focus on information. It doesn't so much move packages as manage data about those packages. It was first to give drivers hand-held scanners and also first to offer full-service "value-web" fulfillment services to e-commerce business customers such as Cisco.

Success in a digital economy demands that you be faster than your competitors, or customers will soon go elsewhere. Business decisions must be made at the speed of thought.

Consequently, every business must become an e-business and the CEO should become the "chief e-business officer."

For a company to develop a speed-obsessed culture and become digitally competitive, its overall corporate strategy must be driven by an e-business focus. This also applies to small firms and non-business organizations of all types.

To be a truly futuristic leader, you simply must "zoom" your organization to the future first.

QUESTIONS to ASK

- How speedy am I?
- How "fast off the mark" is our organization?
- What things or processes do we need to digitize?

THE LAST WORD

TAKE ONE VERB, DAILY

THIS BOOK IS A DAILY DESKTOP REFER-
ENCE. Each and every day, as soon as you
first sit at your desk, reach for this book and
read about one verb.

Do it before you do anything else. It will take only a
couple of minutes while you're waiting for your
computer to boot up. Leave the phone calls and the
e-mails until you have read about the one verb.
Make a pact with yourself that it will govern your
thinking that day. Keep the book open at that page,
within your sight, to remind you of it.

Do that every day, for as long as it takes, until all
26 A-Z futuristic leadership verbs are so embedded
into your executive and entrepreneurial life that
they become second nature to you and the organization you lead.

That's all there is to it. Remember, you are a verb.
Just do it!

ABOUT the AUTHOR

FRANK FEATHER

Frank Feather is a renowned global business futurist, best-selling author, and a much-sought-after public speaker.

- In 1979 he coined the now well-known phrase "Thinking Globally, Acting Locally" which in 1993 he converged into the "glocal" strategy concept.
- In 1980 he was Chairman & Director General of the First Global Conference on the Future, still the largest conference on the future ever held.
- In 1996 he was ranked by Macmillan's Encyclopedia of the Future as one of the "Top 100 Futurists of All Time" - a list that includes Leonardo da Vinci.

Formerly an executive with three of the world's biggest banks, in 1981 he founded Toronto-based Glocal Marketing Consultants. In demand worldwide across all industries, he has advised companies such as GM, IBM, Nokia, and Shell, as well as the IMF/World Bank, the UN, and the US, Canadian and Mexican governments. He's been a Special Advisor to China on economic modernization and market reforms since 1984. Even the world's big consulting firms regularly pick his brain.

Some of Frank's previous books include:
- G-Forces: 35 Global Forces Restructuring Our Future (1989)
- The Future Consumer (1993, re-issued 1997)
- Future Consumer.Com (2000)
- Future Living (2003)

Frank was born and raised in Yorkshire, England, immigrating to Canada in 1968. He is married to Tammie Tan, a native of Shanghai, and they have two daughters, Melissa and Ashley.

Contact Frank Feather directly by e-mail:
FutureTrends2020@aol.com

Notes:

Notes:

Notes: